Aberdeenshire Ways

In November 2013 three artists set off on a six week circular road trip - from mountain to sea and back again - to discover the soul of Aberdeenshire. Their first port of call was Ballater, birthplace of Sir Patrick Geddes, a botanist and pioneering urban planner interested in the relationship between people and place.

The Caravan Gallery, 'a mobile exhibition space and social club on wheels' run by Jan Williams & Chris Teasdale, spent a day or two in eighteen locations to discover how the people they encountered feel about Aberdeenshire today. Starting with an almost empty caravan containing a selection of their own photographs and a large participatory map, they created an evolving exhibition celebrating local distinctiveness with the addition of words, pictures and artefacts contributed by members of the public.

Meanwhile Jacques Coetzer jumped on his bicycle and went to meet key figures of the community representing diverse aspects of life in Aberdeenshire. Jacques' interest in Geddes inspired him to examine how his motto 'think global, act local' applies to Aberdeenshire today.

This publication is a summary of the team's findings and celebrates the unique character of this corner of North East Scotland.

The Caravan Gallery: Jan Williams & Chris Teasdale, and Jacques Coetzer

In Huntly prior to Aberdeenshire Ways tour

Aberdeenshire Ways

a project about regional identity

It's not just about where we live it's about the connections we could be making!

WE HAVE SO MUCH SKY IN ABERDEENSHIRE

Tesco in Banchory "the caravan is standing where the circus elephants used to" :)

ELLON IS ALLEGEDLY HOME TO UK'S LONGEST CAT.

A MILE OF DON IS WORTH TWO OF DEE.

Apparently there is an elephant buried on the B9025 just outside Turriff

Public contributions complemented images by The Caravan Gallery to create an evolving exhibition in the caravan

The Caravan Gallery

The Caravan Gallery is a mobile exhibition venue and arts partnership run by Jan Williams and Chris Teasdale to take art to people and places other galleries might not easily reach. Breaking down barriers and engaging with a diverse audience is intrinsic to their practice.

Jan and Chris are interested in documenting the reality and surreality of the way we live today primarily through photography and social engagement. Since 2000 they have created an extensive archive recording the reality and surreality of life in 21st century Britain and beyond, sharing their observations in specially devised exhibitions in The Caravan Gallery, as well as 'normal' galleries, and in publications.

The Caravan Gallery has travelled thousands of miles and exhibited in hundreds of locations, nationally and internationally, from street festivals to prestigious art and photography festivals, and is equally at home in a supermarket car park as in an international fashion designer's flagship store.

A desire to involve members of the public in exploring regional identity led Jan and Chris to devise their participatory Pride of Place Project model. Part exhibition, part alternative visitor information (where visitors provide the information), photographs by The Caravan Gallery provide the catalyst to get people talking and thinking about where they live. Public contributions responding to the place in question complete the exhibition. Following several such projects in places including Portsmouth, Guernsey, Belgium, Liverpool & Wirral - and, most recently, Huntly where Jan and Chris first fell in love with Aberdeenshire - The Caravan Gallery adapted its methods to collaborate with fellow artist Jacques Coetzer, Deveron Arts and the people of Aberdeenshire on an in-depth exploration of the shire.

Jan and Chris on caravanning in winter:

Many of our photographs in this book were taken in November and December, admittedly a challenging time of year for caravanning in the North East of Scotland, with few daylight hours and people not venturing out so often. Others are a bit more summery. Whenever we've visited Aberdeenshire we've been struck by the extraordinary variety of terrain and culture across the shire and the strength of people's pride in their particular part of it. We realised how unfamiliar many outsiders are with Aberdeenshire, which has been described as Scotland's 'best kept secret' and 'forgotten corner'.

Our Aberdeenshire Ways roadtrip brought us into contact with numerous warm, knowledgeable and articulate people who were generally eager to sing the praises of their shire but were equally forthright in expressing their displeasure when they felt it necessary. We're grateful to the countless inspirational individuals who taught us so much about farming, fishing, fiddling and fly cups, and hope this book succeeds in sharing our discoveries with people across Aberdeenshire. Hopefully it'll persuade some new visitors to come and explore this wonderful region for themselves'.

Visitors to The Caravan Gallery added facts, thoughts and personal observations to a people's map of Aberdeenshire

Jacques Coetzer

Jacques Coetzer is an artist based in the Cape, South Africa, who works internationally. His conceptual approach fuses traditional and new media; social engagement is a key part of his practice and his projects often invite public participation. Much of his work combines visual design and spatial planning and plays out in public space.

He has more than a decade of experience in the research of collective identity, including branding projects with the community of Huntly, Aberdeenshire and the Kilimanjaro Native Cooperative Union in Tanzania.

His exploration of collective identity is holistic, considering a wide and ever developing spectrum of human qualities, as well as our shared relationship with nature and the environment.

On drawing circles and conclusions:

'Being much inspired by Patrick Geddes, the man who so clearly saw the connection between us and the globe we call home, we explored the soul of Aberdeenshire along a circular route that started in Ballater, his birthplace. We soon learnt of the seventy recumbent stone circles in the shire and saw circles and Celtic crosses chiseled out on Pictish stones. Circles seemed to echo out all the way to the ship's steers, buoys and heli deck signs seen in coastal communities today. From people along our way came stories of cyclical patterns in nature and the seasonal migration of salmon along the rivers, connecting mountain and sea.

It was also very rewarding to meet and connect with Geddes' extended family circle on Deeside and in the port town of Peterhead. In Aberdeenshire, we held hands with friendly strangers and danced round and round, all in the spirit of Auld Lang Syne.

From these experiences emerged a design theme that embraces social cohesion, but like the open pattern of the Easter Aquhorthies stone circle, welcomes healthy flow and cultural diversity. Insofar as informing branding and visual identity for Aberdeenshire, the circle motif is primitive and universal enough to contain the ancient spirit of the place and yet so current in the 'local and global' sense that it may hold the social, political and ecological answers of 'now'.

On a much less serious and deliberately random note, the circle becomes a 'fun' lens through which to view Aberdeenshire's pop culture. Spot a circle in the shortbread round, oat cake, Irn-Bru logo, whisky barrel, oil barrel and the shape made by the wind turbine's blades.'

Jacques Coetzer

Jacques and his bicycle checking into a hotel in Peterhead

Seeing life the Geddes way

Scotch thistle

Sir Patrick Geddes (1854 - 1932) was born in Ballater and because of his childhood interest in plants and nature, studied to be a botanist. He co-authored a book on plant life titled *The Evolution of Sex.*

His theories on natural evolution were praised by Charles Darwin, who wrote in a personal letter to Geddes:
'I have read a number of your biological papers with interest and have formed a high opinion of your abilities.'

Charles Darwin (1809 - 1882)

Geddes saw *'creative urge'* as the driving force behind evolution, unlike Darwin, who advocated *'survival of the fittest'* or *'natural selection'* a concept that was anticipated before him by a scientist from Laurencekirk:

Lord Monboddo (1714 - 1799)

In his twenties, during a visit to Mexico, Geddes developed a problem with his eyesight which prevented him from using the microscope. He shifted focus outward and became an urban planner, applying his evolutionary theories on sociology. He formulated the idea of 'organic communities': societies that operate like living organisms.

Geddes was a holistic thinker and wrote aboute the relationship between small things and the universe and man's connection with nature: *'What was decided among the prehistoric Protozoa cannot be annulled by Act of Parliament.'*

In his book *Cities in Evolution*, Geddes developed a term that became synonymous with sustainability and environmental awareness:

Think global, act local

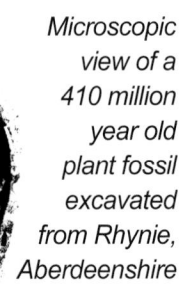

Microscopic view of a 410 million year old plant fossil excavated from Rhynie, Aberdeenshire

RIGHT:
A BALLATER
STREET NAMED
AFTER GEDDES

MRS. SHEILA POTTER AND SON TOM (RELATIVES OF GEDDES), BALLATER

I like to read about my great cousin's philosophies and realise that my own thoughts about the world are not so crazy. He was a peace warrior and a visionary and his ideas are still valid today.

PATRICK GEDDES MEMORIAL GATE, PRIMARY SCHOOL ENTRANCE BALLATER

ALEX GEDDES (RELATIVE OF PATRICK GEDDES) PETERHEAD

I discovered my distant family ties with Sir Patrick Geddes when I attended a symposium on community development and learnt about his legacy.

By leaves we live

'Some people have strange ideas that they live by money. They think energy is generated by the circulation of coins. But the world is mainly a vast leaf colony, growing on and forming a leafy soil, not a mere mineral mass: and we live not by the jingling of our coins, but by the fullness of our harvests.' - Sir Patrick Geddes

RIGHT:
BERRIES ON THE 'GEDDES TREE'
PLANTED BY THE LOCAL COMMUNITY.
BALLATER

Place
Work
Folk

Geddes used the Place / Work / Folk model as a matrix for thinking about the relationship between people and their local environment. The *geography* holds the *resources* that sustain the *people* who live there and these three elements are sensitively connected.

In today's terms it might translate as: Environment / Economy / Anthropology

EASTER AQUHORTIES STONE CIRCLE (FROM NEOLITHIC ERA, 4000 B.C.)
NEAR INVERURIE

Place:
In his own time, the Victorian era of industrialisation, Geddes pointed out that 'place' firstly means 'habitat' or natural environment. He also saw the geographic landscape as the *'theatre of history.'* A place where, through the ages, dramas play out and culture takes shape.

Work:
Economic activity, according to Geddes, is closely linked to the natural resources that sustain it. Aberdeenshire's livelihood has traditionally been associated with agriculture, fishing, tourism and whisky. Oil and gas have significantly added to this since the 1970s and the energy sector is now the primary industry of the shire.

Folk:
Geddes viewed family as the central 'biological unit' of human society from which all else develops. According to him, it is from stable and healthy homes, providing the necessary conditions for mental and moral growth, that come healthy children who are able to fully participate in life. Folk music and dancing helped form Aberdeenshire identity and local traditions have circled out into global culture.

RIGHT:
SINGING AULD LANG-
SYNE AT CEILIDH
EVENING
IN HUNTLY

Aberdeen shire ways

a project about regional identity

'**Aber**' and '**Inver**' are common prefixes in place-names of **Celtic** origin. Both mean '**confluence of waters**' or '**river mouth**' and **Aberdeen** and **Inverurie** are examples. 'Aber' originated from the Brittonic side of the Celtic language, which was in turn influenced by the language of the Picts, who inhabited North East Scotland during the early middle ages. 'Inver' comes from the Geodelic side of the Celtic language, with links to Scottish Gaelic and Old Irish.

The **River Dee** rises in the Cairngorms and flows through Strathdee to reach the North Sea at **Aberdeen**, the 'Oil Capital of Europe'. The general area is called Deeside, or 'Royal Deeside' in the region between Braemar and Banchory, because Queen Victoria loved the place and built Balmoral Castle there. The name 'Dee' appears as early as the second century AD in the work of the Alexandrian geographer Ptolemy. The Dee was originally called 'Deva', meaning 'Goddess', indicating a divine status for the river in the beliefs of the ancient inhabitants of the area.

A "**shire**" is a traditional term for a division of land. The first shires of Scotland were created in English-settled areas in the ninth century. King David the First later created more shires across lowland shores of Scotland. '**Aberdeenshire**' or the 'County of Aberdeen' was established in 1890 and changed to 'Grampian' in 1975. In 1996, the name Aberdeenshire was re-adopted by the local government of the region.

'**Ways**' refer to geographic '**paths**' or '**routes**' but can also mean '**customs**' or '**traditions**'. The **Aberdeenshire ways** project unfolded as a six-week long circular road trip around the shire and aimed to collect the '**ways of the people**' en route.

Aberdeenshire Ways is a collaboration between Deveron Arts and artists Jacques Coetzer and Jan Williams & Chris Teasdale of The Caravan Gallery. Commissioned by Aberdeenshire Council's Be part of the Picture programme.

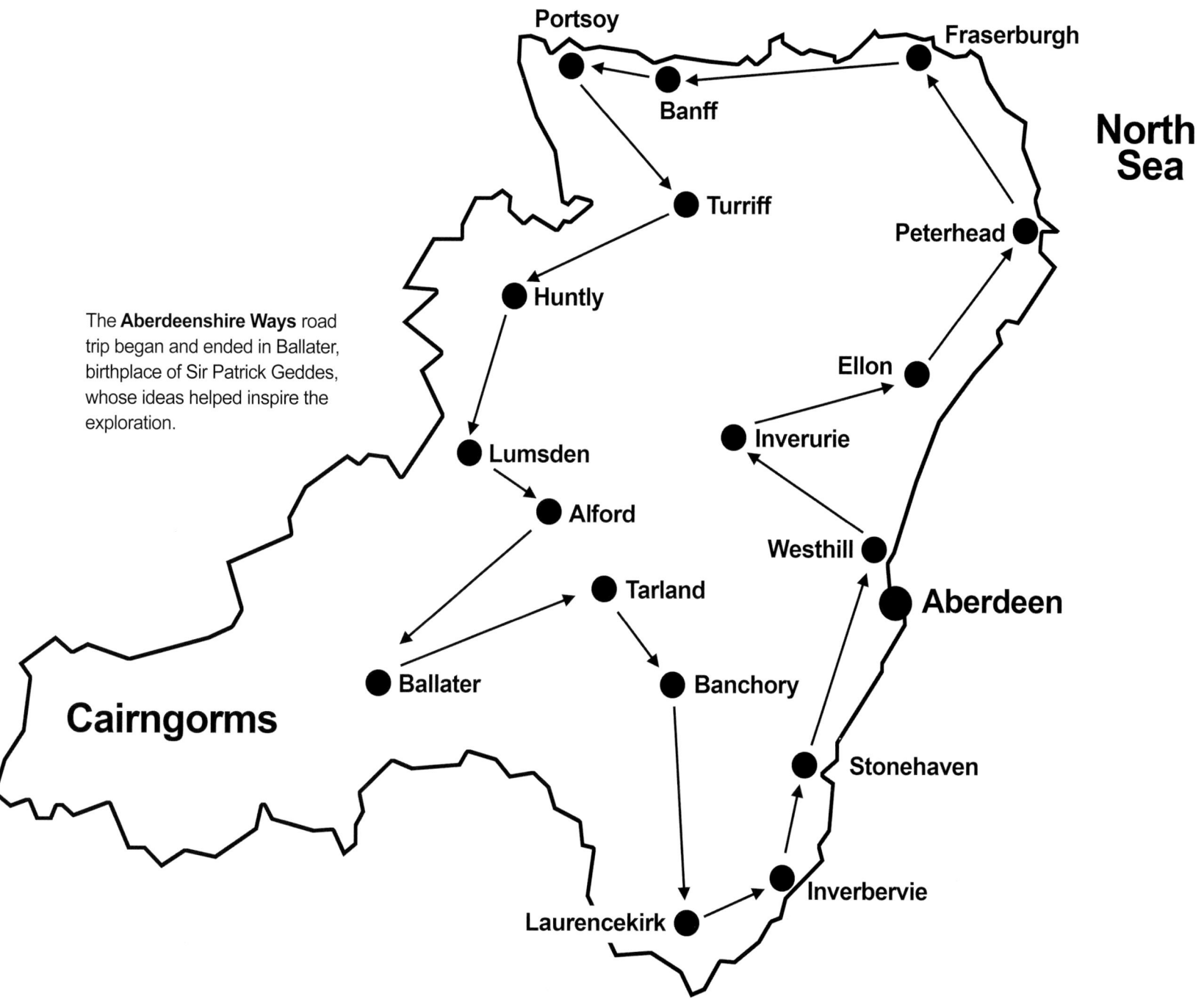

Portsoy

Fraserburgh

Banff

North Sea

Turriff

Peterhead

Huntly

The **Aberdeenshire Ways** road trip began and ended in Ballater, birthplace of Sir Patrick Geddes, whose ideas helped inspire the exploration.

Ellon

Inverurie

Lumsden

Alford

Westhill

Tarland

Aberdeen

Cairngorms

Ballater

Banchory

Stonehaven

Laurencekirk

Inverbervie

From mountain to sea

The 'Valley Section' was one of Geddes' methods to analyse geographic region according to occupations that it sustained. The illustration on the right is based on one of his studies from the early 1900s, while the one below represents Aberdeenshire a century later.

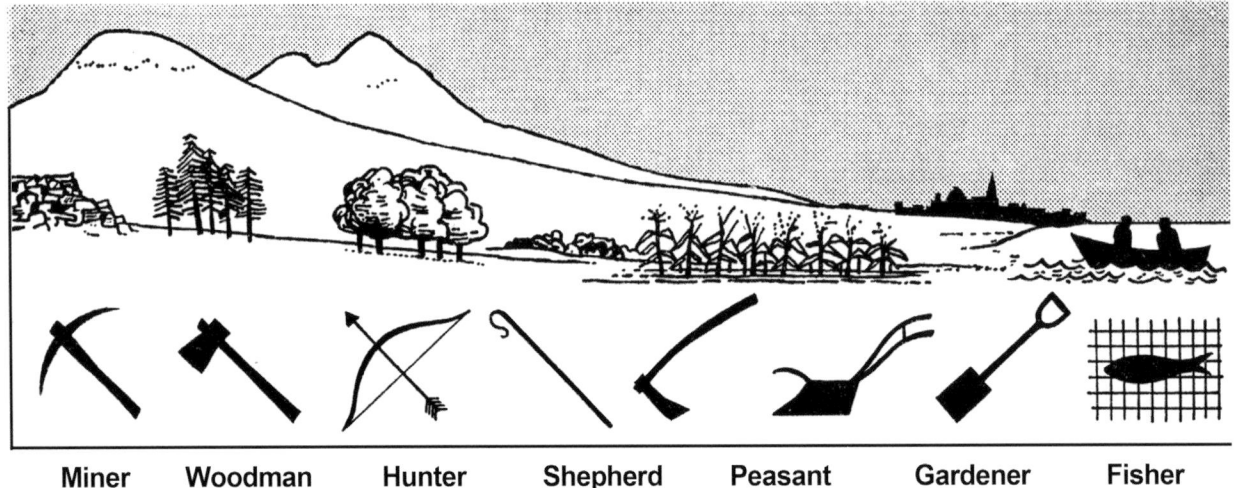

| Miner | Woodman | Hunter | Shepherd | Peasant | Gardener | Fisher |

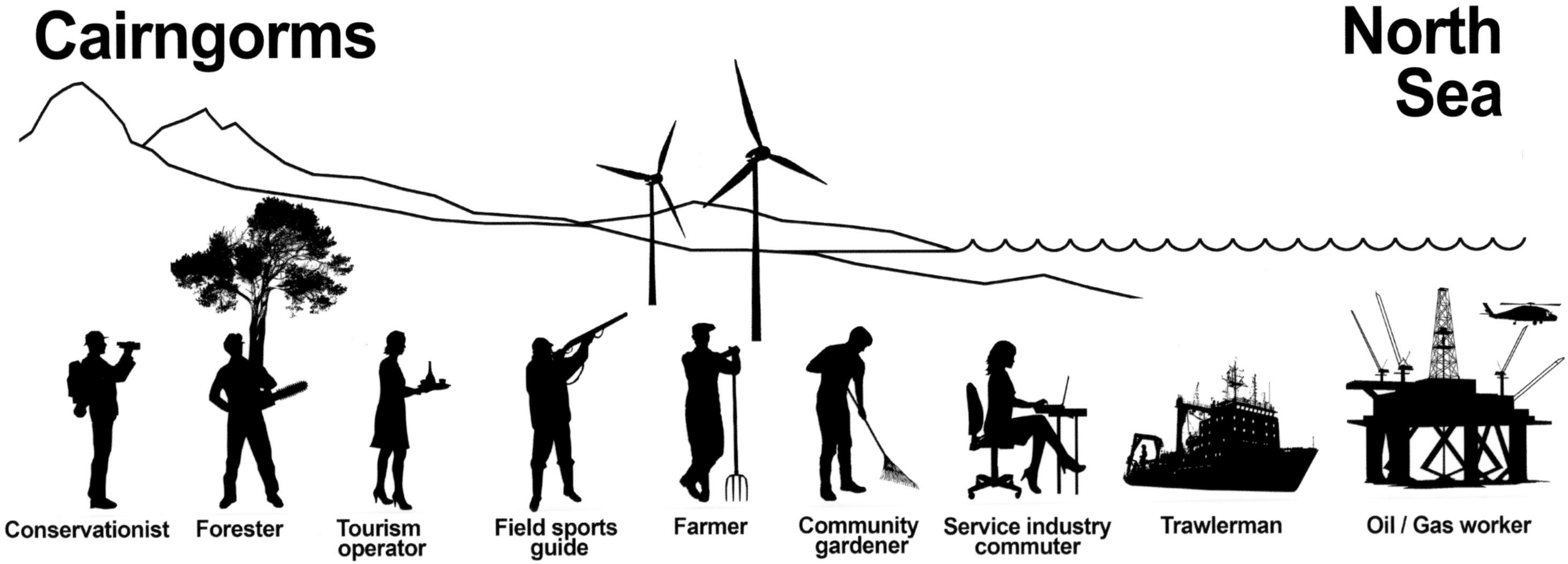

Cairngorms

North Sea

| Conservationist | Forester | Tourism operator | Field sports guide | Farmer | Community gardener | Service industry commuter | Trawlerman | Oil / Gas worker |

View of River Dee near Lyn of Dee and Mar Lodge Estate

Looking back at Cairn O'Mount on road to Laurencekirk

Foghorn at Kinnaird Head, Fraserburgh

Ballater
The Capital of
Upper Deeside   In the Shadows
of Lochnagar.

for deer roam & folk bide
granite buildings sparkle in
the Sun. Golden oak leaves
hung on just now 'fore the
frost.. There's snaa!
on Lochnagar!

Ian Murray

Tel: +44 (0) 2392 877415
Mobile: 07808 160207
e-mail: admin@thecaravangallery.co.uk

www.thecaravangallery.co.uk

ASDA, Smithdown Road, Liverpool

Paul Smith Space, Tokyo, Japan

Bath Abbey, Fringe Arts Bath

Poem given to us by local writer Ian Murray

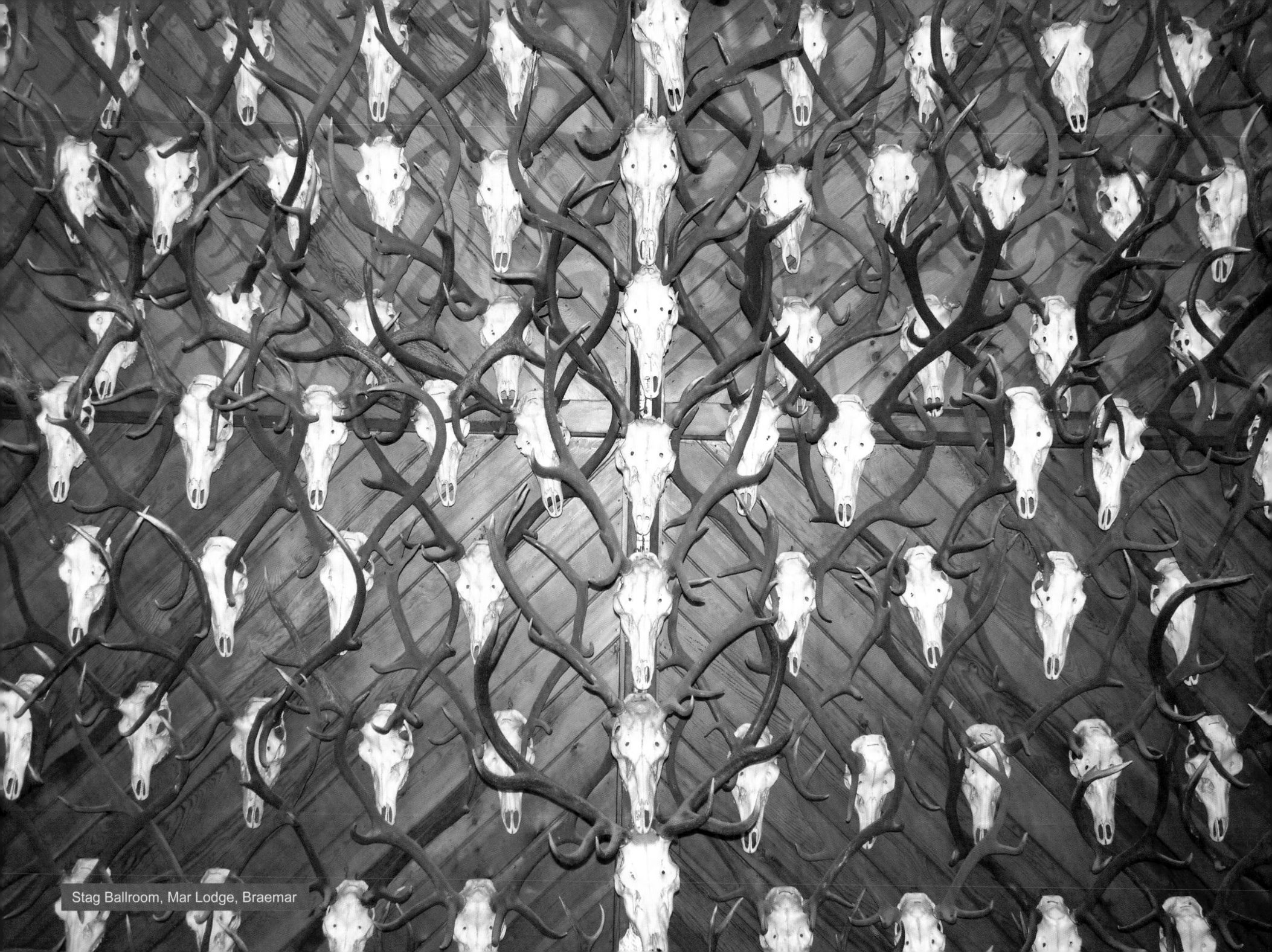

Stag Ballroom, Mar Lodge, Braemar

The Cairngorms means
'The Blue Mountains' but
the Gaelic name for the
same mountain range
translates as the
'Red Mountains'

'The last bow and arrow
battle happened on
the Ballater pass

In Dinnet in the victoria
restraunt there is a ghost that
sets the tables, changes the
music and plays with the
Lights.

Photo of Braemar Gathering & Highland Games; Bridge over River Dee to Mar Lodge

Drinking fountain near Ballater

Patchwork deer in cafe, Braemar

Deer bell

Rustic timber pillars, Braemar

Royal Warrant sign on shop in Ballater

Before going into battle fighting members of a clan each placed a stone on a pile which formed a cairn at the place point of muster. After the fight, survivors removed their stones from the cairn leaving behind a smaller cairn as a memorial/ reminder of the numbers slain.

Macbeth Arms, Macbeth Square, Macbeth Cairn, Macbeth well Macbeth was allegedly killed in a battle in 1084 ish. His head was cut off just off after the battle. There's a stone at the side of the field.

MACBETH -RELATED

TARLAND:

'The butcher says they all buy their meat online these days. I like to prod it and sniff it!',

Last speaker of Aberdeenshire Gaelic Norah MacDonald. She stayed in Cutaway Cottage (corner of the cottage was sliced off to make way for railway)

Gordon Highlander memorial, Tarland

Mysterious sculpture in wall of pub car park, Tarland

Restored AA Box 472 on A93 at Cambus O'May

Ecclesiastical bird box outside church in Banchory

Ravenswood Royal British Legion Club, Banchory

stagecoaches horses kept there and

Gallowhill MORE CAR PARKING School Charles Murray educated here

URGENTLY REQUIRES

The Greatest Doric Poet

Very Heavy Snow!! ...it's higher up

Welcoming

o Muggarthaugh Hotel

Moved 2

French Kate haunts this place

Craigievar Castle

Kittie Rankie was a witch, lady's maid from France (French Kate)

DISNEY style

HOWE OF CROMAR

All of it should be in the National Park

The home of Paul Anderson

Yes!

YES yes!

Real heritage but no one cares

Tornoveen Cat Sighting

Big Cat

EXODUS TO ALFORD Stanley Robertson travelling musician

CRAIGIEV - INSPIR FOR CAS

Queen's View

TARLAND

Queen Victoria's house was outside arland

MIGVIE CHAPEL!

ROB ROY'S

CAVE

'It needs more shops!

Tarland is big enough No more houses!

Tarland is big enough Macbeth buried here

WHERE'S LUMPHANAN

2 witch here (Jea

ⓧ Tom naverie

Cows with guid end'ers

Macbeth was brought bay and hacket doon in the woods around here

Torphi

CAT TLE IN ROCK

FORMA Battle of Culblean

Gilderoy McGregor

HOWE OF CROMAR - a bowl shaped view

Black Faced Sheep coffee shop

OSPREYS

'Burn o' VAT

it's strath kirk (+Reel)

Aboyne

'bunking off school and sitting in the heather

GRUMPHA MAN HA

The War

Craigievar Castle near Alford

View from road over Cairn O' Mount

Cairn O' Mount road in mist

It is irritating for us Kincardineshire people to be lumped in with Aberdeenshire. We are immensely proud of our heritage in our ancient county.

Laurencekirk is one of the few places left where people still say hello in the street.

Cheeky truck and electric vehicle charger, Laurencekirk

Sunset Song

LEWIS GRASSIC GIBBON

MODERN CLASSICS

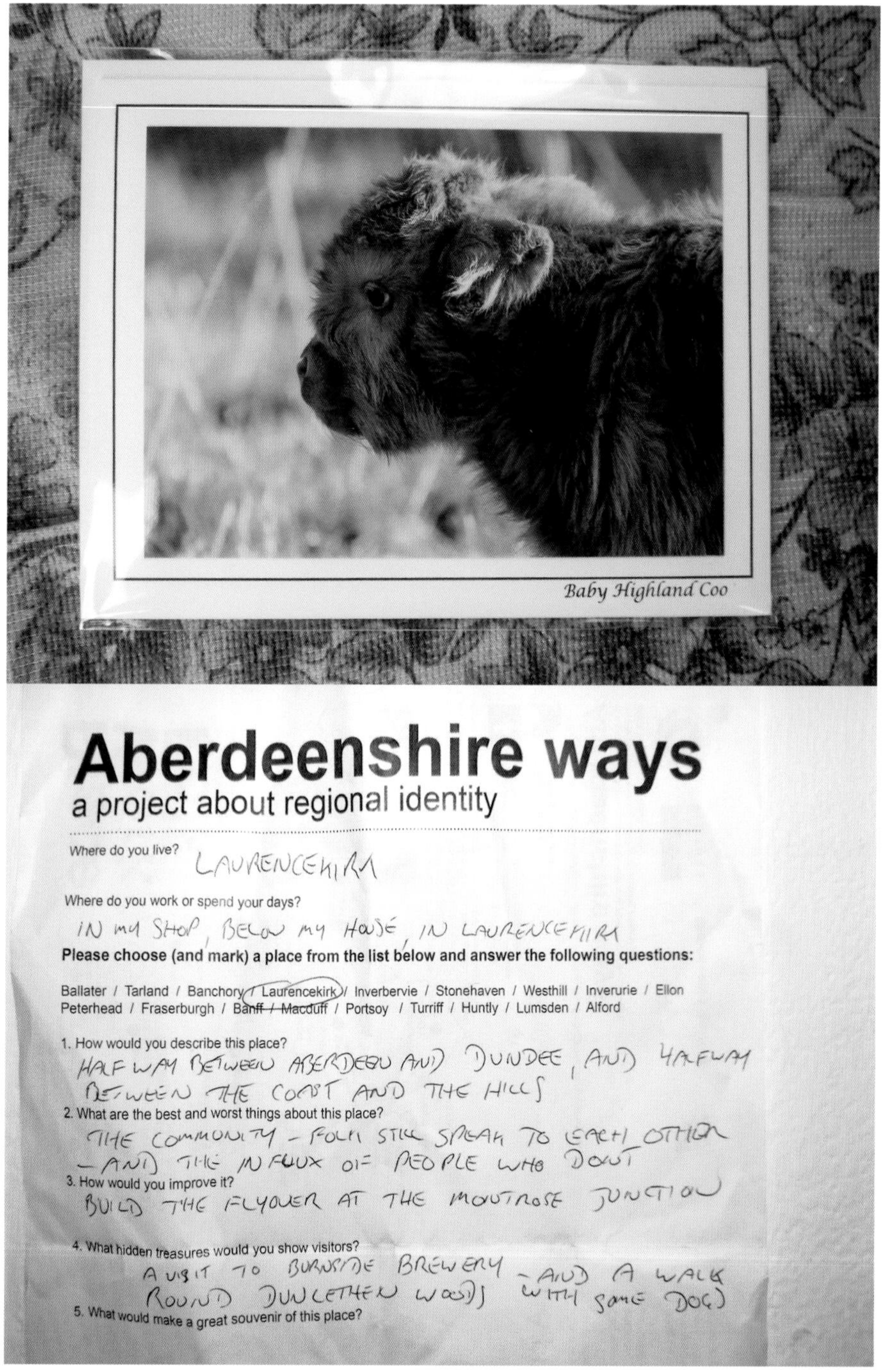

Baby Highland Coo

Aberdeenshire ways
a project about regional identity

Where do you live? LAURENCEKIRK

Where do you work or spend your days?
IN MY SHOP, BELOW MY HOUSE, IN LAURENCEKIRK

Please choose (and mark) a place from the list below and answer the following questions:

Ballater / Tarland / Banchory / Laurencekirk / Inverbervie / Stonehaven / Westhill / Inverurie / Ellon
Peterhead / Fraserburgh / Banff / Macduff / Portsoy / Turriff / Huntly / Lumsden / Alford

1. How would you describe this place?
HALF WAY BETWEEN ABERDEEN AND DUNDEE, AND HALFWAY
BETWEEN THE COAST AND THE HILLS

2. What are the best and worst things about this place?
THE COMMUNITY - FOLK STILL SPEAK TO EACH OTHER
- AND THE INFLUX OF PEOPLE WHO DON'T

3. How would you improve it?
BUILD THE FLYOVER AT THE MONTROSE JUNCTION

4. What hidden treasures would you show visitors?
A VISIT TO BURNSIDE BREWERY - AND A WALK
ROUND DUNLETHEN WOODS WITH SOME DOGS

5. What would make a great souvenir of this place?

Memorial to Hercules Linton, designer of the Cutty Sark, Inverbervie

Garden, Inverbervie

THE OLDEST SMALLEST THING TO
HAVE WALKED ON EARTH CAME
FROM COWIE JUST NORTH OF
STONEHAVEN WHERE A 1¼ INCH
FOSSIL WAS DUG OUT OF THE ROCK.
IT WAS A 450 MILLION YEARS OLD
MILLIPEDE.

There's more going on in
Stonehaven than you think!

MEARNS FM

based under Town Hall
in Stonehaven. Biggest
community radio station
in the world covering
250 miles

STONEHAVEN OUTDOOR Pool

THE LAST HEATED OUTDOOR POOL IN

SCOTLAND.

42

Skatepark, Stonehaven

Visitors to The Caravan Gallery in Inverbervie

Free flour, Inverbervie

Skateboarding mosaic, Stonehaven

SLUG Rd

very scenic

Rickarton

Raederkos Roman he was Gent.. great improver

BARCLAY OF URY

URY ESTATE

Lifted donkey over a wall

reclaimed bogs so crops could be grain

Lots of people from here went to Corby work in the steel works

Little Scotland

Sketey Shop

OUL SidE

One of the best pieces of fish ever - the BAY

occasional Robert Burns Wed gannets Round here.

SAT IN

THE HAAR

the oldest smallest thing to walk on earth came from Cowie

OPEN AIR POOL

THE HIGHLAND BOUNDARY FAULT

ideal Open Air Sunbathing Sp on Gallows Hi

ung he bobbins There was a village which they said TOCHTY they took allest + friendliest Highland Games in wee valley

Lovely Seaside!

We have a skatepark

INK-BOTTLE HOUSE

Stonehaven

no more silver darlings

Sunbathing Sp

THE EWEL houses)

There was two dung middens on at each end of the village and the villagers would skite from one the villagers out to the other!

NO DENTIST IN STONEY

20p for a wee here

FOLK FESTIVAL 2nd W'END JULY

BAY CHIPPIE - No. 1 in Britain

DRUMLITHIE (SKITE) Robbie Burns used to come to my house at his dols.

Deep Fried Mars Bars

Ice Cream Shops

GLENBERVIE old church where Rabbie Burns Taylor Who d Ceylan as from here

Home of the famous Fire BALLS

Auntie Betty's Ice-cream shop ♡♡♡ Fantastic Hot Chocola

CASTLE

JOAN EARDLEY WAS 'ERE

- DO get the extra toppings.

relatives are buried feathes Circular Cycle ride.

The Whigs Vault + The Lions DEN on the Crown Jewels

DUNNOTT

CATTERLINE GALA 2nd WEEKEND IN JUNE

Faughls.. bird sanctuary

GILLYANGO'OS (SP!) SWEET SHOP

AUCHENBLAE field of flowers

OUR

46

Painting displayed at The Creel Inn, Catterline

Public art on the seashore at Stonehaven

CARRON
FISH & CHIPS
1-3 ALLARDICE STREET
STONEHAVEN
VAT No. 888 958 328

BATTERED MARS BARS   1.50
-ALL SALES   1.50--

SUBTOTAL   1.50
CASH   1.50

SARAH
#001-009-0006-0001 13/11/2013 13:12-R

THANK YOU FOR YOUR
VALUED CUSTOM
PLEASE CALL AGAIN

Deep fried Mars Bar in the chip shop where it was invented in Stonehaven

Stones on the beach at Catterline

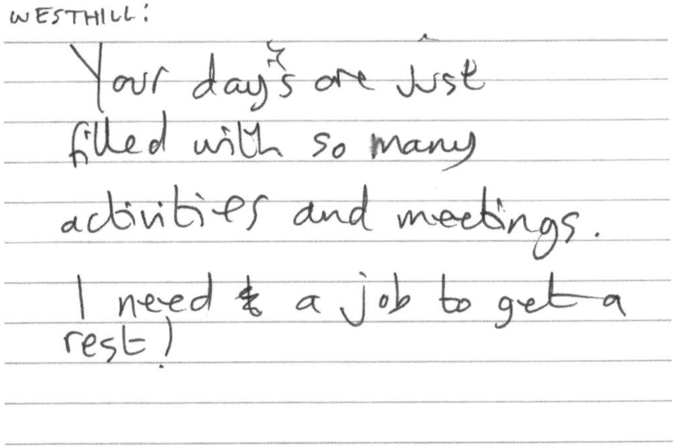

WESTHILL:

Your days are Just filled with so many activities and meetings.

I need to a job to get a rest)

An enthusiastic member of the Westhill 50+ Group

This post box has been painted gold by Royal Mail to celebrate
Tim Baillie
Gold Medal winner
London 2012 Olympic Games
Canoe Slalom: Men's Canoe Double(C2)

Gold painted post box to honour Olympic gold medal winner Tim Baillie of Westhill

Imposing conifer in the park at Westhill

River Don at Inverurie

Bennachie from East Aquhorthies stone circle

MANY CHILDHOOD MEMORIES
OF THE SHAKKIN BRIGGE
BURNHERVIE.
ADULT TIME SPENT MAKKIN
OATCAKES SKILL PASSED DOON
THE GENERATIONS

Next day delivery?
Not when you've got
an AB postcode!

INVERURIE

'we counted at least 20
cafés and tea shops. Some
of them are in jewellers
(Sinclairs), furniture shops
(Andersons) and the one in
the garden centre's mobbed'

'I've just had a massive dinner
at Morrisons'

Pen No: 321
Farm Assured Status: FA

Quantity: 11
Breed: CONT
Type: LAMB

Wt kg Qty Avg kg
644   1   644

Livestock auction at Thainstone Mart near Inverurie

Circular seating arrangement on the banks of the River Ythan, Ellon

'It's not just about where we live it's about the connections we could be making!

Mobile fishmonger comes to your door, great if you can't get down town.

Yum Yums are exquisite!

Only made better by adding Bacon.

ELLON

Coat of Arms of Baillie Gordon; voucher exchanged for lifesaving chili hot chocolate in Ellon

Last Bus Cafe, New Pitsligo

Ellon.

Ya've got to go to the Last Bus café in New Pitsligo. It's worth it if you can find it!

ELLON IS ALLEGEDLY HOME TO UK'S LONGEST CAT.

My grandfather was a fee'd horseman in 1914, and got paid £1 a year. He was given a slice of cold porridge from the dresser and a boiled egg on Sundays.

Slains Castle ruins overlooking Cruden Bay near Peterhead

Sand dunes and beach at Balmedie

Ornamental fountain at Trump International Golf Links, Balmedie

Trawlerman in Peterhead

Illuminations depicting trawler and oil rig, Peterhead

Staff at The Trading Post, Peterhead, which specialises in local crafts and produce

PETERHEAD FISHING FLEET USED TO LEAVE 1 MINUET PAST MIDNIGHT ON A SUNDAY TO AVOID SAILING ON THE SABBATH

Blue moggins — (fae the bloo toon)

Hose made by fishermens wives for their husbands to wear at sea. Every toun made moggins in a different colour. Anyone lost at sea could be identified by their toun of origin

In the 70's the young affluent fisherman were always buying new cars, we used to say they changed them when the ashtrays were full.

Doric barometer from The Trading Post, Peterhead

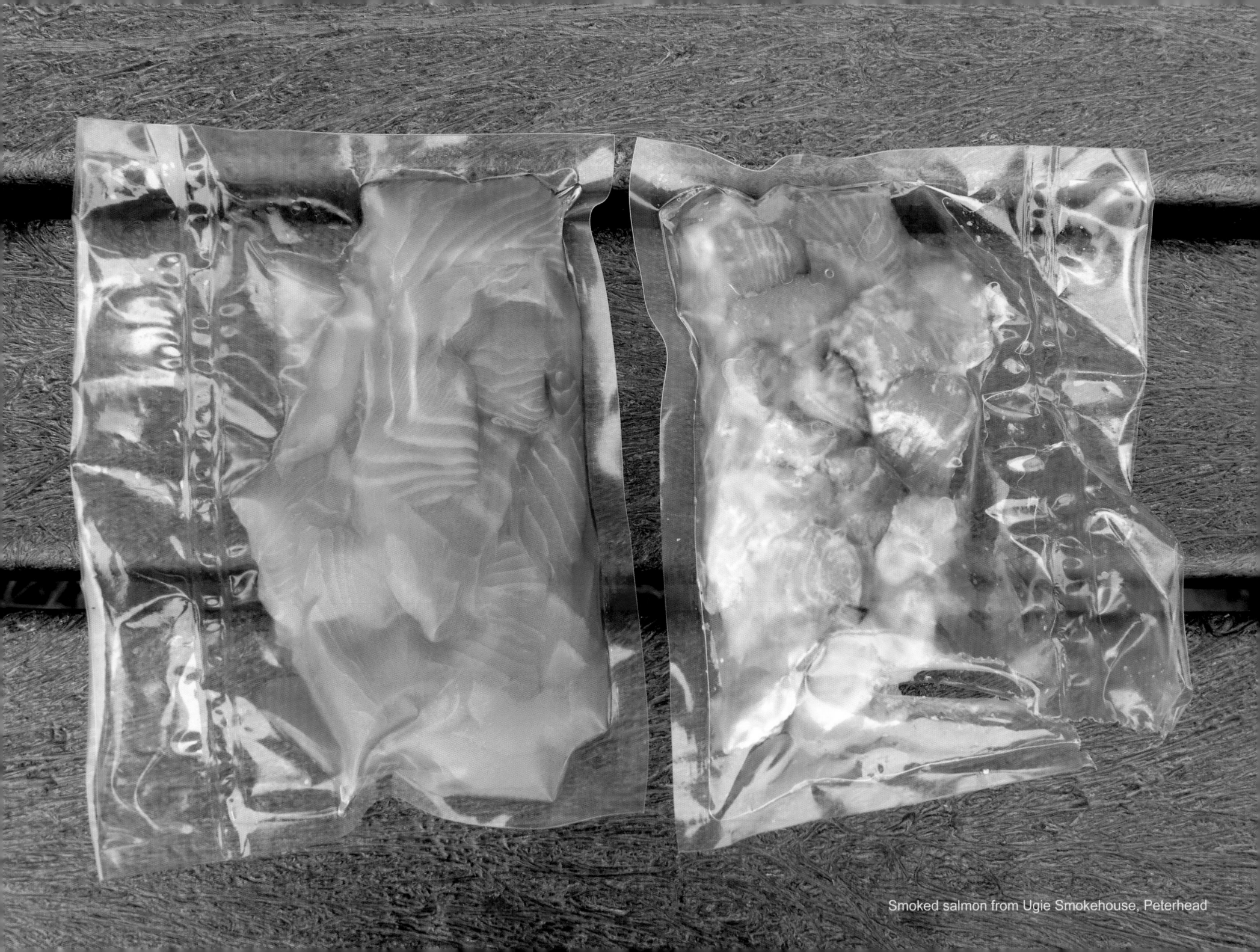

Smoked salmon from Ugie Smokehouse, Peterhead

Mintlaw

RORA MOSS

PEAT

ST-FERGUS MOSS

Viewing tower on saplinbrae estate

My auntie owns it! :)

great
...SKIFE
...IN UK. G

TRADITIONAL FARE.

APPY PLANT RDEN CENTRE.

Fishwifie stable with a wee girl

Glenugie Distillery 'ya'll need an interpreter up there'

CIRCO MODO

LONGSIDEAIRFIELD

the people are so friendly
CLOSED TOWN

BLING TOWN

Good smoked fish cakes
in chipper
at Adachouse
Great
Graveyard
Ellon 20/11/13 : this is a summer day in Peterhead. Wait till you go there!!

MORE CHURCHES THAN PUBS!

Wetherspoons

John Ironside says its good for cycling

Peterhead

Fabulous Arbuthnot museum house

Blue Mogner (socks) POSITIVE

THE BLUE TOON

Fish suppes at the Dolphin cafe I wouldna go there!

Believed to have approx 250 individual religious groups

PRAISE THE LORD.

1 shop 1 post office

Cruden Bay

history started 1012 "Battle of the Danes"

Best karate club i Scotland

LONGHAVEN CLIFFS

FERGUS CEMETERY

NORTH LEFT END CONNECTION

'PIRATES' airport (RAF) here

CRIMOND the name of the hymn tune for 23rd psalm The Lord is My Shepherd

Biggest white fish port in Europe the fish head south when shows coming

OLDESTSMOKE HOUSE IN SCOTLAND

DRUGS & BRETHREN

SEALS in harbour

BONNIE BUCHANHAVEN SCURRYS!

MAMBO'S NIGHTCLUB.

Boddam they don't talk to the Boddamers each other the monkey hung

Bullers of Buchan views great

Prison then & Now, nice Area!

SLAINS OLD LODGE CASTLE

BIGGEST WHITEFISH PORT IN

BEWARE THE SCURRIES!

YES FOOD!

NOOOO!

PETERHEAD

Nature on the Doorstep

Enterprise from the sea

UGIE SMOKE HOUSE
OLDEST SMOKE HOUSE IN SCOTLAND
BUILDING USED FOR THE SAME PURPOSE
FOR THE LONGEST PERIOD OF TIME IN
SCOTLAND

Fisher Jessie statue and fisherman, Peterhead

FRASERBURGH:
The accent in Peterhead is their own. They've got a different language to us. We talk more like people in Motherwell than they do even though they're just down the road. Ya ken?

FRASERBURGH

"Mince + TATTIE Soup"

Fraserburgh:

' I love it here. I'm from London. I've got a budgie. The sun shines everyday. It's quiet here. I love it '

Fish processors, Fraserburgh

69

Sorting out fishing nets at the harbour, Fraserburgh

Trawler, Fraserburgh

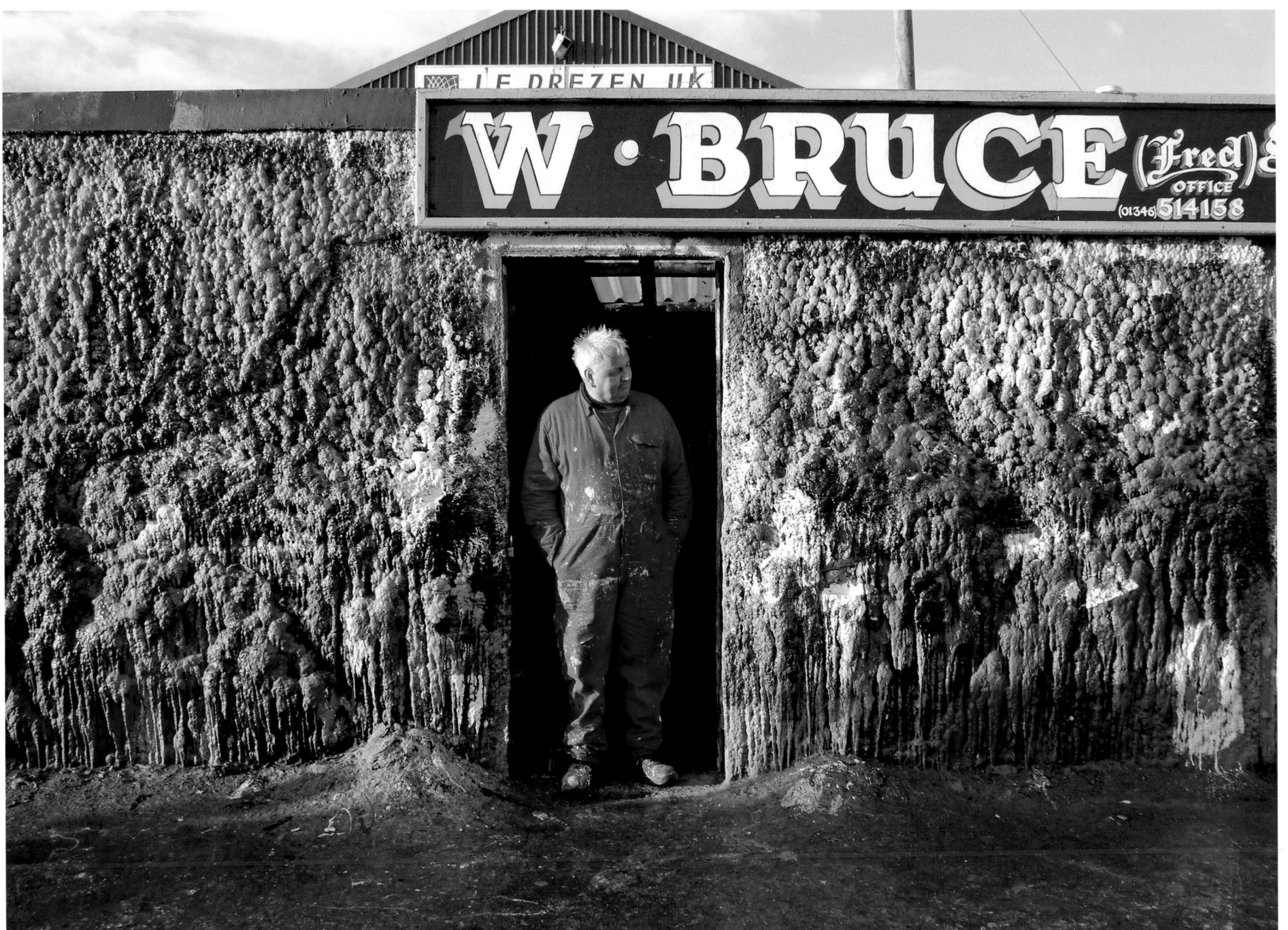

Ship painters in Fraserburgh

Fifty shades of grey in Fraserburgh

Harbourside at Rosehearty near Fraserburgh

Seafaring tableau in cottage window at Rosehearty

Pennan

Crovie, Gamrie Bay

Dog waste bin, Gardenstown

Gardenstown harbour, Gamrie Bay

View of Moray Firth from Gardenstown

Gannet colony at Troup Head

Hermit lived in cave

FAB PANTO IN PORTSOY

Annual BANFF / STAVANGER YACHT RACE

EAST HEAD Fairyring Brilliant

fireplace £storeshop

another language doon there!

dochty

(finechty) coun try

Portknockie
PTK Sunnyside Fantastic Soup

Beach Findlater made Castle here I know would used over

DOOCOT5PORTS
had to WALK
DRAGON'S TEETH Pigeons and is 6-700 yrs old

WHITEHILLS community benefit WINDMILL shore

Best ice cream EVER!! 55/

Cullen

PORTSOY

path

Annual Petanque Comp. on New Years Day

Officially the best ice-cream

May Queen of Scots Handmaid is buried here

Sardine Sandend

FORDYCE

tunnel

new favourite place

GREAT COMMUNITY Sailing festival

rocks

ROCKS

rare plants butterfly

BOYNDIE remains aerodrome

+ MEMORIAL + CASTLE

A pine marten on birdtable

Home of footballer Iain Jess

Home Jimmy McBeath

SCOUT

Standing Stone

RS
COFFEE

VISIT GARDENS OPEN DAY IN JULY CAR BOOT SALE ONCE MONTH

Super little Castle Warm Microclimate

TURBI

SOY

* * SCOUT

the ga

Tarlair art deco tidal open air swimming pool (now closed), Macduff

Spotty Bag Shop, Banff

Banff Harbour was a very busy place in the days of sailing ships, a few of them being in port when this photo was taken.

One of the two cottages on the left, No. 17 South Castle Street, which stood opposite Castle Lane, was a former Banff Post Office. It was here that Mr John Fraser, postmaster, received mail with the news of Waterloo.

BANFF - fisherman

£1000 take home pay
in late 70s + early 80's
Money spent in 2-3 days
in pubs, women, gambling etc
weekend started on Thursday

BANFF:

If you want to make a
cake you have to drive all
over the place to look for
ingredients. If you want an
avocado pear you have to
drive to Elgin

BANFF:

Go to the Ship Inn
for real ales but
cover your ears

Piper Findlater
1st VC awarded in First World War
from Banff.

Piped for a battle — immediately
had his legs shot from under
him but managed to sit on
a rock + pipe for the battle

Fish names are different along the coast
Haddock :— Powie / Haddie
Dogfish :— Blin 'hai
Cod :— Wary Codling (young one)
Scorpion fish :— Tilly Gimper (Fraserburgh)
            Mugie Bisarr
            Jocky Gundy
Porpoise :— Louper Dog / Macduff Man's Whale

PUELLY
A gull in Banff

BANFF'S THE PLACE.

BANFF BRIDGE STATION

D. R. LESLIE

"Banff is unequalled for sunshine and temperature . . . You could go for
long periods in a state of nudity."—Provost Stephen, Banff, on Monday.

[Nelson, British Columbia, Monday.—Two hundred and forty Doukhobors have
been sent to prison for participating in nudist demonstrations. Some may be de-
ported at the end of their sentence.—Reuter.]

Portsoy

17th century harbour, Portsoy

Portsoy Harbour — JIG

paulina smith-Hong
2004

PAULINA SMITH

BOAT FESTIVAL

PORTSOY MARBLE
SERPENTINE (GREEN)
USED FOR TWO CHIMNEYS
(FIREPLACES) IN THE PALACE
OF VERSAILLES!

PORTSOY ICE CREAM
WE MAKE OVER 100
FLAVOURS + SORBETS
AND ITS ALL
HOMEMADE

PORTSOY FAIRIES
Unnamed volunteers
maintain coastal paths and
old Portsoy lookout post.
There's a fairy ring b/wn Portsoy &
Whitehills (impassable 2 yrs ago) so
we've done major work. Collected
washed up oil drums to make picnic spot
in the gorse. There are divining rods
and there's a visitors book.

Net poles on drying green in front of Salmon Bothy, Portsoy

Turra Coo sculpture at Gateway Community Centre, Turriff

Stone relief on St Congan's church ruins, Turriff

Drainpipes and sandstone walls, Turriff

Tap O' Noth vitrified hill fort near Rhynie

HUNTLY

Weed Farm

Cyurcy

fine martens

A96

Rothiemay Standistones.

GHOSTLY & CARRIAGE!

LOOK OUT FOR FOGGIE MAN

met at school around here

TRANQUILITY
WILD WEST Tour.

Drumbair House turn

I go horse riding around here!!

Views

CAIRNAGAT COFFEE SHOP.

Baucicht cemetary with Victorian Angels

first hydro-electric scheme in Scotland

Red Bridge
part of old Tay Bridge

was Ronald Centre here!

Huntly CASTLE.

Strathbogie Monument

home of Deveron Arts

Bogie's Bonnie Belle

Haggi Hunfin

BIRTHPLACE of GEORGE MacDONALD

allotments unhappy our productive!!

POPULATION OF HUNTLY HAS REMAINED ALMOST UNCHANGED FOR 200 YRS

James Croll's commercial disaster which led to success in Olympics in cycling

AT GARTLY HOME OF THE BEST LIVE FOLK.

nordic ski stones

DEANS SHORTBREAD
'is the best'

Icon — we get your women brew ice cream
↓ tasty

KENNETHMONT

Distillery Ardmor Kee

WILD Farms!

LOTS OF SKIING
IN THE WOODS

Source of Deveron

The Tap A Noth

St. Marys Stone

Uganda here

Missionary from Rhynie who walked 2.5 years to Lake Victoria

GARTLY MOOR PRODUCED THE SLATE FOR THE ROOF OF BALMORAL.

WARD HOUSE previously owned by the Gordons, now Gonzalez

Noruite

Btaz sherry

Leith Hall
'Hanging' Tree

River Deveron, Huntly

Free shortbread from Dean's of Huntly; Rizza's ice cream shop, Huntly; Gordon Highlander patch on leather biker's jacket

Inscriptions on facade of Huntly Castle

Embroidery by artist collective Rhynie Woman based in the village of Rhynie

All the villages round here had a country hall. No electricity, no water, no sanitation, just a bucket in the corner. We never got ill then. If there was any trouble Blue Peter (the police constable) would come along on his Norton bike. You could hear him coming but he wasna allowed in. He was a huge man with large boots. You couldna sit down after he'd dealt with you.

The hall's closed, only a month or so ago. The site's been sold for development.

An Aberdeen Angus coo

* Workshop.
International Crystal Healing
* Academy

about 2000 people killed in an afternoon

BATTLE
Jacobean
EXTREMELY HISTORIC
BUT NOT WIDELY
KNOWN
UNFORTUNATLY

enemy of

PREMNAY - something

Sluie Hill

Craigievar film club

Tullynessle

Alford Oatmeal at
Montgarry Mills, oldest
working mill in Scotland

Murray Park

Charlestown Country

DORIC CENTRAL

More NORTH

Best Place to Live

KEIG

Doric accent in early

Bennachie

Good Pub in
Premnay (Hynes
Moony and
visit Luckleyhead
Castle.

GADIES
Restaurant

FOLK Singing
MUSIC

Fin Bennachie pits on its
the Geerie lads will get a d

Sore circle
bond
group.

Awesome!

The Railway came
in 1859

in flatstones
R. Don

Haughton
Hotel
originally
Railway
Hotel
stagecoaches
horses kept
there and

Centre of
drove roads

friendly

Welcoming

into this place

NEED MORE CAR PARKING

HAYS
lemonade

GRAMPIAN
TRANSPORT
MUSEUM.

Alford

URGENTLY REQUIRES
MORE CAR PARKING

Gallowhill
School
Charles
Murray educated
here

Very Heavy
Snow!! it's higher
up

Charles Murray
The Greatest
Doric Poet

Bilbo's
Blue Tonymusk
Sik-o-menask
Norman church
Fab hills
for riding
cycling!

Moved to Alford
2 years ago
and want to
live here the
rest of my life

OFFICIAL
BUT VERY
it's A

Castle
was a witch,
since

OMAR

Yes!

YES

Real Heritage
but no-one cares.

Muggarthaugh
Hotel

Big

Tornoveen
Cat Sighting

CRAIGIEVAR

INSPIRATION

BIG
CAT
IN THE
WOODS AT
BACK OF
ANNIE'S

Public artwork in Alford

Idea

ABERDEEN ANGUS FESTIVAL.
IN ALFORD.
'HOME of THE ABERDEEN ANGUS'

ALFORD AFTER 15 YEARS
WOULD NOT GO BACK TO ABERDEEN
FOR ALL THE TEA IN CHINA

Graeme Barber
butchers is a must
visit in Alford!

Ballater Girls dump boyfriends before the arrival of Queen for guards and policemen / You can't improve perfect / Billy Connolly has a pile of Rangers top in his cupboard and my dad accidently knocked them all over (when he was working in his house). **Tarland** Contemporary local hero is fiddler Paul Anderson, who continues to make a hugely important contribution to continuing the North-East fiddle tradition of Peter Milne, Scott Skinner etc. / Paul Anderson is a world class fiddler who hasn't forgotten his roots. Does his best to promote local music and talent / Did you know all the shops here are run by women? / BALMORALITY: the art of slavishly copying the ludicrously feudal pretensions encouraged by the Royal Family. **Banchory** My local hero is the farmer opposite who never stops / Barclay of Ury, a 7ft man from Stonehaven, ran 1000 miles in 1000 days. **Laurencekirk** A perfect little corner of Scotland / The Arbuthnott manuscript was painted and illuminated in Arbuthnott church and is now in Paisley Museum / The call centre for Oyster Cards is in Laurencekirk. **Inverbervie** A lot of history and a lot of hidden treasures and stories to be told / Hercules Linton & Joan Eardley for her paintings of wild seas of Catterline / We have been waiting so long for a skatepark that we are starting one ourselves / Check out the North East Folk Archive. **Stonehaven** Festivals, folk and fireballs / Dunnottar / Stonehaven is a few degrees south of the Capital of Alaska / Hamish Henderson was a great man for collecting folk songs, stories and traditions. He's buried up at Glenshee. Jimmy MacBeath was a Portsoy Travelling singer - James Stewart, Scottish Traveller, musician and author of 'Deeside Tinkers' / Fred's Threads' is a newsletter by Frederick Stewart the 'Heritage Mannie' from Porthlethen Heritage Society which meets regularly in the library. **Westhill** Local writer James Fiddes has written a history of the area / Men's Shed / Westhill Art Project / For stone circles Julian Cope's 'The Modern Antiquarian' has a good coverage of the area / I did some transcriptions for the North East Folk Archive / Pauline Cordiner is a Scottish Soryteller who sings bothy ballads. **Inverurie** Stewart McBride writes about psychos in Aberdeenshire / Hannah Miley made us all proud by getting to the Olympics / When I was young (many moons ago) Doric words were forbidden! Now it is positively encouraged / I can feel earthquakes (from Bennachie) in my house/ Bring your own Mars Bar to Meldrum Fish Bar & they will batter & deep fry for 50p. **Ellon** Stanley Robertson - recently passed away, but he was a Traveller and he shared his stories and songs in a magical way / I only moved here two years ago but it's home, more than any other place has been / We're forgotten north of Aberdeen. It's all about the Central Belt as far as the government's concerned / Annie Lennox's mother lived in Ellon / They d'a hae lemons in Aachnagatt. **Peterhead** the Bloo Toon / Bloo moggans – Peterhead fishermen's hose / Good history, bad weather and scurries / community spirit / We should promote three themes for the town: harbours, heritage and history / The 'Old Pretender' landed here in 1715. He was only 26 / Fetterangus = Fishie: Local folk clubbing together to buy a wind turbine. Puts a whole new slant on things / Nature on the doorstep, enterprise from the sea / the fish cooked straight off the boat is like nothing you can buy in the shops - superb! / 32 different religions in Peterhead.

Fraserburgh Bring Daniel O'Donnell to the Broch! / Very multicultural / Friendly but hard folk / Best beach and fantastic windsurfing championships / Bonnie lighthouse / first solar powered telephone box / Cherry Cocking Capital of Scotland / Myaar means gull here **Banff** The Banff & Macduff Christmas Lights Association brought us together / Lord Byron was the coarse loon of Banff / When we go there for our groceries it's like going on holiday / If you want to make a cake you have to drive all over the place to look for ingredients. If you want an avocado pear you have to drive to Elgin/ Puelly: a gull in Banff **Portsoy** People have a love for their town, for its heritage too. They are friendly and welcoming to new residents and Portsoy has a real community spirit / The stories, that is what makes a place a place / I'll take the high road and you'll take the low road and I'll be in Scotland afore you' – I hear this tune being sung in my house at night by ghostly men's voices harmonising / A nice window of weather. No midges / Skip 2 the Beat: Scotland's first competitive skipping club / Salmon Bothy, Boat Festival, Folk / Portsoy Fairies: unnamed volunteers who maintain coastal paths and old lookout post **Turriff** A place where farming and agriculture dominate, and a sense of community is still very much alive / Tractors in Tesco car park, farmyard aromas wafting around town / Local Vocals: A folk group of local women perform anywhere / singing local songs of farming and fishing at nursing homes and for local groups. We sing for our tea / Some of the best communities are in Buchan. Can- do ethos / I'm glad I didn't go to university because I went offshore instead. **Huntly** Beating Heart of Gordon Country / What makes buildings, groups and people special is their interconnectivity / Plenty of Room to Roam / Huntly is the home of the fly cup (where else can you get a coffee and buttery and top up for £1.50 while socialising and raising money for local charity!?) / Nordic ski centre, farmers' market auction mart cafe and Dean's Bistro / In the mid-19th century large crowds gathered near Huntly castle to hear gospel preaching / Tranquillity near Glendronach is a Wild West Town, the only replica of a Western Town in Scotland. The site is home to the northern Rough Riders Group **Rhynie** sp (Ruh-hynie) sp (Ruh-hine) is famous for cinnamon buns. Rhynie means a very royal place as Pictish royalty lived here / Rhynie Man – a carving on a stone – stands in the reception area of Woodhill House in Aberdeen / Ryhnie used to have 2 tailors, 2 butchers, 2 garages, bakers, 1 barbers, 1 jewellers, 3 or 4 sweetie shops, grocers and chemists, 2 pubs, 2 banks, 2 chip shops **Lumsden** Gateway to the Cairngorms / Scottish Sculpture Workshop / Touching the Sky / my near perfect home, on border of farmland and hill. Rural with strong links to the past, true and honest, little spoilt by materialism and commercialism. Friendly but reserved and gentle, unassuming and self-sufficient. Beautiful, peaceful and raw. Vulnerable and fragile / A strip with nice views /Quiet, isolated, rural, community pride and lack of influence from commercialism. It is beautiful. It is desolate **Alford** Emeli Sande has done a great job globally and still keeps to her roots / Charles Murray, the greatest Doric poet, is very much underrated / All of the Community Hospitals in Aberdeenshire are connected to Aberdeen Royal Infirmary (ARI) by videoconferencing.

Balls, beakers, buoys, baskets and barrels

Patrick Geddes called geographic landscape the *'Theatre of History'* - a place where, through the ages, dramas play out and culture takes shape. Here are some round shapes from historic and contemporary Aberdeenshire

400 carved stone balls (petrispheres) were dug up between the Dee and Deveron.

Vessel used by people of the Beaker culture, early inhabitants of Aberdeenshire

Easter Aquhorthies stone circle

Iron age round house

Pictish symbols of salmon and circles in Kintore Kirkyard

Celtic crosses with circles were carved on some Pictish stones

Fisher folk symbol from Peterhead

Coracle boat at the Portsoy Boat Festival

Seaman's mission pulpit with symbolic ship's steer

Highland dancing

The artist Joseph Beuys said that Celtic culture united nature and spirit

Auld Lang Syne circle

RIGHT:
STONE BALLS IN MUSEUM COLLECTION
AT MINTLAW

Global exports

Bred by Hugh Watson, William McCombie and Sir George Macpherson-Grant

Scottish craft brewery, BrewDog, originated in Fraserburgh and their beers are now loved in the UK, America, Scandinavia and Japan

Butter shortbread rounds from Dean's of Huntly, who export shortbread to 30 countries around the globe

Gavin Sutherland's 'Sailing' was recorded by Rod Stewart in 1975 and sold more than a million copies in the UK

First official logo of the BBC, when Lord Reith of Stonehaven was the founding director

RW Thompson's air tyre

James Taylor of Laurencekirk, founder of Ceylon tea industry

Twiggy in a Bill Gibb dress

King scallops from Fraserburgh, the biggest shellfish port in Europe

Aberdeenshire single malt whisky

The 40-gallon whisky barrel was the most common container used by early oil producers

LEFT:
WHISKY BARRELS

Local fare

Vegetarian haggis is now found in selected Aberdeenshire butcheries

Turnips are called 'neeps' and North-East Community Radio is called 'Neep Radio'

Alford oat cakes

2014 is the celebration of Rizza's of Huntly's 100th year of Italian ice cream making

Aberdeenshire tatties (potatoes)

DERREK FORREST, OWNER OF THE BERVIE CHIPPER, INVERBERVIE

The fish supper is ever popular and earns us a living in the countryside. We moved here from Glasgow - it is a good place to raise children.

Butteries were invented to stay fresh at sea

The IRN-BRU logo. The orange-coloured soft drink is an Aberdeenshire favourite

RIGHT:
SCOTTISH SALMON AND SCRAMBLED EGGS
AT THE BOAT INN, ABOYNE

Iconic red phone box associated with the film Local Hero, much of which was set in Pennan

Local heroes

Annie Lennox, international pop icon, HIV Aids activist and philanthropist

'Dummy Jim' Duthie made a bicycle trip from Fraserburgh to the Arctic circle

Emeli Sandé grew up in Alford and her shaved look was created by her Jamaican hair stylist in London

Jimmy 'Scout' MacBeath, bothy balladeer from Portsoy

Billy Connolly, comedian

Dame Evelyn Glennie, percussionist

The Royal Deeside is still strongly associated with Queen Victoria

Filmed in Pennan in the 1980's

Fishwives used 'skull baskets' and creels to carry fish to inland towns

Jim Patterson from Portsoy, trombonist of Dexy's Midnight Runners

Thomas Glover's Japanese love affairs were the inspiration for Madame Butterfly's 'Pinkerton'

Old and new Aberdeenshire icons

'Aberdeenshire turrets'
Balmoral Castle

Balmedie golf ball

Oil platform heli deck sign

Ploughing matches, held in Alford

In order to avoid working on the Sabbath,
fishing boats would leave Peterhead harbour
at one minute past midnight on Sundays

Salmon fly reel from
Turriff Tackle shop

Old Portsoy buoy factory

Boy racer culture

Sporran with Celtic knot design

Inverurie Loco Works
Football Club was founded
by railway workers in 1903

Logo associated with
archaeological sites
in Aberdeenshire

According to National Health Scotland,
teenage pregnancy rates in the shire are
lower than in other parts of Scotland, in
correlation with fewer deprived areas here

BARLEY BALES NEAR BANFF

KINNAIRD HEAD, FRASERBURGH

FOCUS ON A JOAN EARDLEY PAINTING IN THE CREEL INN, CATTERLINE

GIANT BUOY ON ESPLANADE, FRASERBURGH

Natural cycles

Moray Firth moon jellyfish
in Macduff Marine Aquarium

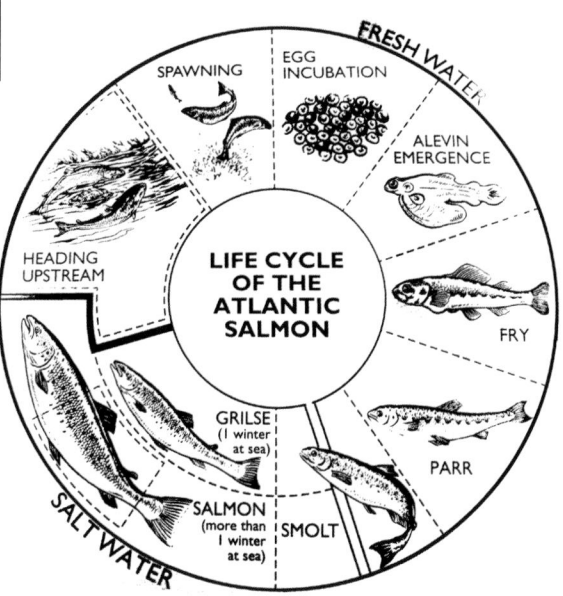

LIFE CYCLE OF THE ATLANTIC SALMON

FRESH WATER

SPAWNING
EGG INCUBATION
ALEVIN EMERGENCE
FRY
PARR
SMOLT
GRILSE (1 winter at sea)
SALMON (more than 1 winter at sea)
HEADING UPSTREAM

SALT WATER

DR. ADAM WATSON, BIOLOGIST, ECOLOGIST, MOUNTAINEER - BANCHORY

John Muir said everything in nature is connected - The salmon's life cycle is a beautiful example of this, linking our rivers with the sea.

TRAWLERMEN AT PETERHEAD FISH MARKET

CLAIRE MATTHEWS, MANAGER OF MACDUFF MARINE AQUARIUM

For Scotland's Year of Homecoming, we are planning to focus our youth program on the cyclical migration patterns of marine animals.

Local and global, the Aberdeenshire way

When you embark on an adventure to map the soul of a place, it helps to have a 'spirit guide' - someone to give you clues and point you in the right direction. For us, this wise man came in the form of Sir Patrick Geddes (1854-1932), the visionary botanist and urban planner who coined the term 'Think global, act local'. He was born in the Deeside town of Ballater, where our artistic enquiry into Aberdeenshire ways started. It was there, on day one of our project, that two of Sir Patrick's relatives, Mrs Sheila Potter and her son Tom presented themselves to us. We had lunch and a long talk and then Tom took us for a walk to show us Sir Patrick Geddes Way.

Our team was keen to get the full picture of the place and its people. Patrick Geddes, who was the inventor of urban planning's regional survey, inspired us with his desire 'to see life whole'. His geographic analysis of region considered every natural habitat as a microcosm of the greater universe, yet his down-to-earth Scottish outlook realised that the people who settled on the land also had to make a living there. This flowed as an undercurrent in many of the conversations we had with the hundreds of people we met in the towns we visited. Perhaps most notably so in the fishing ports of the North, where serendipitously, another relative of Sir Patrick just "appeared" in our little yellow caravan. Alexander Geddes runs a community upliftment program called Positive Peterhead that would have made his great uncle proud. We are now Facebook friends with Alexander and his project is one of the many volunteer-based economic initiatives that we found on our Aberdeenshire Way.

Patrick Geddes also defined the geographic landscape as a 'theatre of history'. This gave us a meaningful way to look at the layers of archaeology embedded in the soil of North East Scotland, starting 410 million years ago with primitive life forms fossilised in the Rhynie Chert. Later came the first signs of human settlement by people of the Beaker Culture, in the Neolithic age (4000 - 2000 BC), with their enigmatic stone circles associated with the moon and the seasons, and of which there are more than 70 in Aberdeenshire. Also from the same era, more than 400 beautifully carved stone petrspheres, the size of tennis balls (purpose unknown) and all dug up in the land between the rivers Dee and Deveron. Enter onto the historic stage the Picts with their standing stones carved with symbols of salmon, deer and cauldrons. Later came Christian influence and circular Celtic crosses began to appear on some of these "stanes", like the Maiden Stone, near Inverurie. Pictish brochs, hill forts, tower- and round houses made way for medieval castles, of which there is a long list (fifty plus) to be found in Aberdeenshire, with Balmoral as crowning glory.

But perhaps the humble bothies hold the most important key to the soul of Aberdeenshire folk: the bothy ballads that originated amongst the farm labourers were the handiest tools of oral history. Alan Lomax' 1960s recordings documented some of these musical stories, as sung by Jimmy 'Scout' MacBeath, a Scottish traveller from Portsoy. Traditional Aberdeenshire songs like "The bonnie lass o' Fyvie" (Peggy-O) was gently carried out across the world by Folk musicians like Bob Dylan and Simon and Garfunkel. Rod Stewart took local Peterhead lad Gavin Sutherland's song 'Sailing' around the world in the seventies. Also consider the singing of 'Auld Lang Syne' and the customary holding of hands at the end of a friendly ceilidh evening and how far that tradition has circled out across the globe.

The phrase 'from mountain to sea' contained in the current Aberdeenshire Council motto is very appropriate as the beautiful valleys and rivers of the shire are integral to the cultural landscape. The motto also significantly connects to Geddes' Valley Section model, which illustrates the interconnection of man and nature. As in Pictish folklore, the Rivers Dee, Don, Deveron, Ythan and Ugie can be seen as life- giving veins that run through the shire, connecting the inland communities with the North Sea and its economies of fishing, oil and gas. Even more significantly, the life cycle of the Scottish salmon in these rivers is symbolic of a beautiful local and global migration that perpetually occurs with the changing seasons. These fish swim up the Aberdeenshire rivers to spawn and in time, the young return to the open sea. Some make it past the nets, trawlers and oil rigs and follow the currents all the way to Iceland to return to the rivers in a season or two. They navigate back to where they started their lives as little fingerlings. When we met Dr. Adam Watson, another one of Aberdeenshire's wise men, he explained how the life cycle of the river salmon forms part of a larger synergy with the otters and the freshwater pearl mussels, to form a bio-diverse whole. It was another Scot, John Muir, who said: "When we try to pick out anything by itself, we find it hitched to everything else in the Universe."

A few weeks later we were shown around Macduff Marine Aquarium by the manager, Claire Matthews. For Scotland's Year of Homecoming, she and her staff are planning to focus their youth programme on the cyclical migration patterns of marine animals of the Moray Firth. She explained that part of the reason for the aquarium's existence was to create public awareness of Aberdeenshire's sensitive sea and river ecosystems. A section of the beautiful aquarium also houses displays of local culture and the language of the North East fisher folk. Claire envisions finding a balance between marine conservation and commercial fishing in Scottish waters.

In an audiovisual display at Fraserburgh's Museum of Scottish Lighthouses and heritage centre, we heard the Doric voice of an old fisherman who proclaimed that "Scotland is married to the sea". This is certainly true for many of the Aberdeenshire folk who are still involved in the fishing industry, however much that has declined over past decades. Some locals still continue the strong fishing tradition and considerable numbers of crew from the Philippines and Eastern Europe have added a global nuance to the culture of contemporary Aberdeenshire. In Portsoy we met two friends who decided to make their living on the sea. Mark (30) kept to the local tradition of his family and is the skipper of a fishing boat that operates from Fraserburgh. His friend Tom decided to work offshore and now makes his living on oil rigs across the globe. Emma, Mark's sister, is a childcare manager and at the friends' pub farewell introduced us to a local favourite, the turquoise 'refresher bomb' cocktail. The next day Mark and Tom would both set off to sea.

Not far from Portsoy is the tiny cove village of Pennan, where the classic 1983 film 'Local Hero' was made. The plot is central to Aberdeenshire culture and the issues sound familiar, even today: Global, corporate oil company strategies versus a small town community's dwindling local traditions and values. It all plays off against the backdrop of a windswept and endangered Scottish coastline. The story ends well and the equilibrium is restored as a result of the local hero's tenacious attitude and the big businessman's awakening to the mystical Northern Lights. How would such a drama play out today and what would be the 'Aberdeenshire Way' to balance the current debate around Donald Trump's golf course development and its ecological and cultural impact? In the towns we visited there were many unsung heroes who were actively involved in getting things done locally. This ability to organise communal action seems to be inherent to North East Scottish communities. Revisit the Turra Coo story and next time you are in town, buy 'Totally Locally Turriff ' goodies.

It turns out that quite a few Aberdeenshire folk have been influential across the globe, especially during the expansion of the British Empire. As we visited towns and heritage societies around the shire we learnt of Glover, the Japanese industrialist, Thompson, inventor of the pneumatic tyre, Taylor, who established tea in Ceylon, Stevenson, the lighthouse builder, MacDonald, the fantasy writer, Lord Monboddo, the early evolutionist, Legge, who translated Chinese writing, MacKay, missionary engineer of Uganda, Forbes, the financial journalist who founded Forbes Magazine, Grassic Gibbon, the socialist writer, Lord Reith of the BBC, and so the list grows. Contemporary global stars in the making include the singer Emeli Sandé from Alford, who was named a hero in our surveys. Stars of Aberdeenshire's economy still include well-loved export favourites like single malt whisky, shortbread and Aberdeen Angus beef. Perhaps the most uncelebrated Aberdeenshire hero of all is Patrick Geddes, who is known internationally as the father of urban planning. Everywhere but at home, his ideas have stayed evergreen and are relevant more than ever in post-modern thinking.

The term 'Think global, act local' comes from Geddes' book 'Cities in Evolution' (1915) but became popular in the seventies, with the rise of the green movement. The slogan has been used in various contexts, also as strapline for the first Earth Summit in Rio in 1992 and by many people, including Kofi Anan, Paul McCartney and Yoko Ono. Yet, the very nature of what it means still rises above that of an over-used cliché. Through the course of this project it became clear that Patrick Geddes' holistic methodology is very applicable to the world that Aberdeenshire finds itself in today. The positioning of a place within the wider economic reality is precisely why branding projects exist. From Geddes' pen also came the words "megalopolis" and "conurbation" to describe the huge, overpopulated cities that rural Aberdeenshire's "room to roam" is very possibly the perfect alternative to. Our surveys showed that many local people, especially those who have come from cities elsewhere, value the clean air, rivers, beaches and rural walks offered by the area and this is in sync with Aberdeenshire's current status as one of the best places to live in the UK.

The Caravan Gallery enabled us to engage with Aberdeenshire communities at street level and we heard about real issues from real people. Said Geddes: 'Local character' is thus no mere accidental old-world quaintness, as its mimics think and say. It is attained only in course of adequate grasp and treatment of the whole environment, and in active sympathy with the essential and characteristic life of the place concerned." We were thus pleased to read how Francois Matarasso's findings in the "Pinning Stones" reflected our own experiences: "It is easy to make connections with the everyday concerns of Aberdeenshire people about how to conserve a unique environment and its high quality of life in a changing world, whose pressures range from the cost of petrol and empty shops to wind turbines and post-oil economy ... They are existential problems faced by humanity globally that have to be responded to locally."

And so Aberdeenshire's heart lies open, like a circle of granite under a big Northern sky. At once heavy and dreich, like a grey Sunday morning, and light as a fiddle reel. The North East of Scotland is a special place and perhaps its enigmatic soul refuses to be defined. Artist Joseph Beuys called the Celtic world "a light from the West" and found here enough philosophical space for spirit to embrace earth. A place where you can be local and be global. A place where you can "be".

Jacques Coetzer

Themes and Location Shots

The following pages take a closer look at themes including:

- the Doric language
- food and drink
- music and leisure activities
- renewable energy
- history and archaeology

A further selection of photos shows The Caravan Gallery and visitors in each location.

The team was unable to visit Lumsden due to road closures so went to Rhynie instead.

A Doric sign on a bench in Huntly: if you're weary and have sore feet, rest a while and take a seat

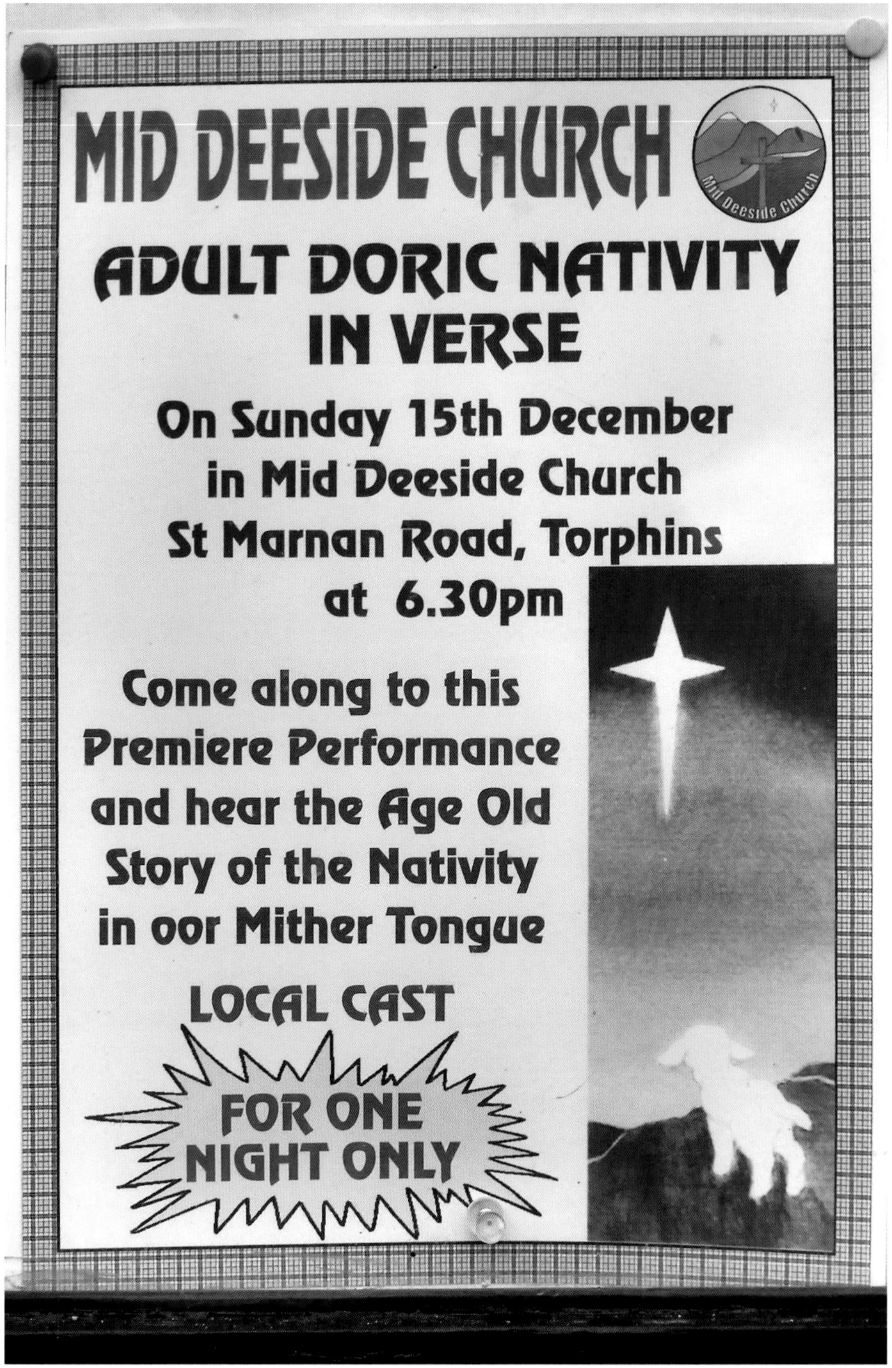

Posters in shop windows advertising Doric entertainment and a Doric New Testament

"THE FOWK
AN' THE LAN'
THE LAN' AN'
THE FOWK"

NEEP

(North East Ethnic
Person)

Come awa in!

It's gran ti see ye!

I SPEAK DORIC ON FACEBOOK.

FAR WID WI BI WIDOOT A WER FREENS ON F/BOOK
FAE A DWER E LAN.
FAE SANINE, BUNFF

FICHERAN

FIT U FICHERAN AT?

STRUSHEL LUMP

PERSON IN A MESS
BEDRAGLED.

A Doric speaking Scotsman when
called up for service:

' I understand you so
it's up to you to
understand me'

From a Lancastrian incomer!

Fit like?

Nae bad, nae bad ken. Charvin
awa.' Foo's yersel?

(Best I can do)

(They teach Doric in schools now)

A bag of chips:

A PYEOKE O'

CHIPS!

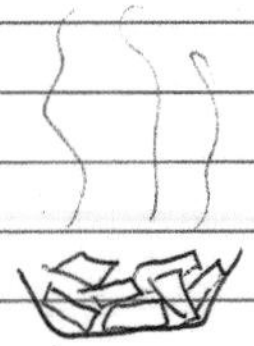

'She seems
quite young
to be Doric'

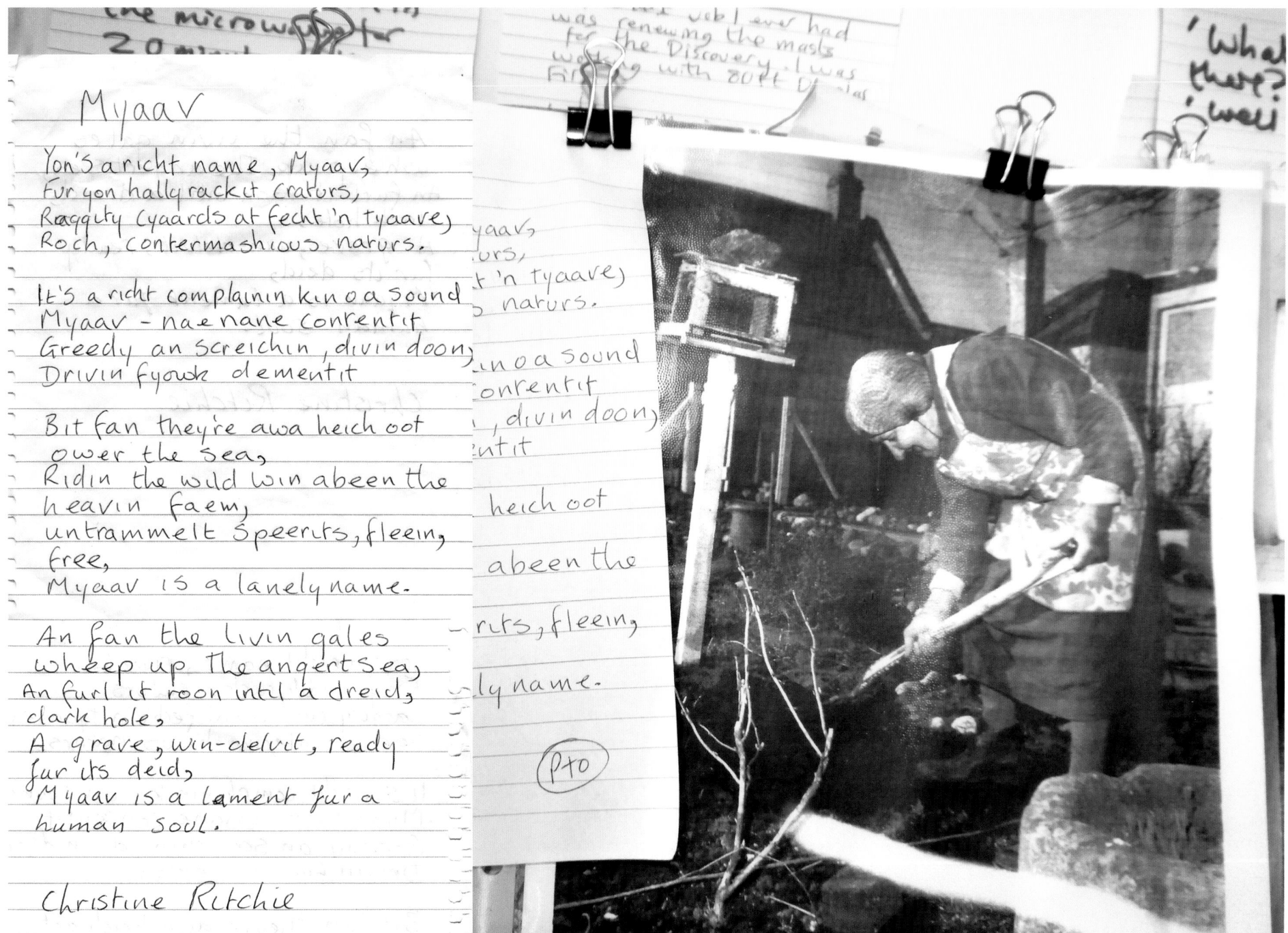

Myaav

Yon's a richt name, Myaav,
Fur yon hallyrackit craturs,
Raggity (yaards at fecht 'n tyaave)
Roch, contermashious naturs.

It's a richt complainin kin o a sound
Myaav – nae nane contentit
Greedy an screichin, divin doon,
Drivin fyouk dementit

Bit fan they're awa heich oot
ower the sea,
Ridin the wild win abeen the
heavin faem,
untrammelt speerits, fleein,
free,
Myaav is a lanely name.

An fan the livin gales
wheep up the angert sea,
An furl it roon intil a dreid,
dark hole,
A grave, win-delvit, ready
fur its deid,
Myaav is a lament fur a
human soul.

Christine Ritchie

125

ABERDEENSHIRE:

You are now
entering
Buttery country

Buttery Festival

The Buttery was "invented" by Aitkens Bakery in Torry, Aberdeen. It was developed to store well and to reheat several weeks or months later to fresh condition for fishermen to eat

Rothiemay Outdoor Bowling Club
Coffee Morning
Saturday 20th July 2013
Stewarts Hall
10-till - 11-45am
Adults £1.50p   Children 80p
Various stalls.

Buttery Morning

Saturday 7th December
2013

Peterhead Trinity Church

10am -12noon

£2.00

(IN AID OF CANCER RESEARCH UK)

Relay For Life

Together we will beat cancer

Butteries in Rhynie

Angus Roast Beef Roll
served with creamy horseradish sauce

Angus Steak Burger
served with fresh fried onions & thick Scottish cheddar slice

BIG Angus Steak Burger with Sliced Angus Steak
served with thick Scottish cheddar slice & fresh fried onions

Cabrach Venison Burger
served with cranberry & port jelly

Robbie Burns Haggis Burger
served with fruity chutney

Succulent Breast of Chicken Burger

Veggie' Burger
served with spicy fruity chutney

Stovies with beetroot in Alford

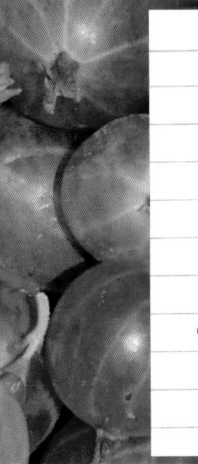

PORTSOY ICE CREAM
WE MAKE OVER 100
FLAVOURS + SORBETS
AND ITS ALL
HOMEMADE

RECIPE FOR
ABERDEENSHIRE TEA:

A kelly kettle

A fine view

A good companion

And a decent river

You don't get a
'piece' with yer
fly cup in England.

I LIKE HEALTHY, LOCALLY
SOURCED FOOD WASHED DOWN
BY REAL ALE / FRUIT JUICE
AND A WEE DRAM.

A FISH SUPPER IN GOURDON
DOESN'T GO AMISS!

BEETROOT:

stick it in a dish in
the microwave for
20 minutes with cling
film on top of the dish
then peel it. You keep
all the flavour!

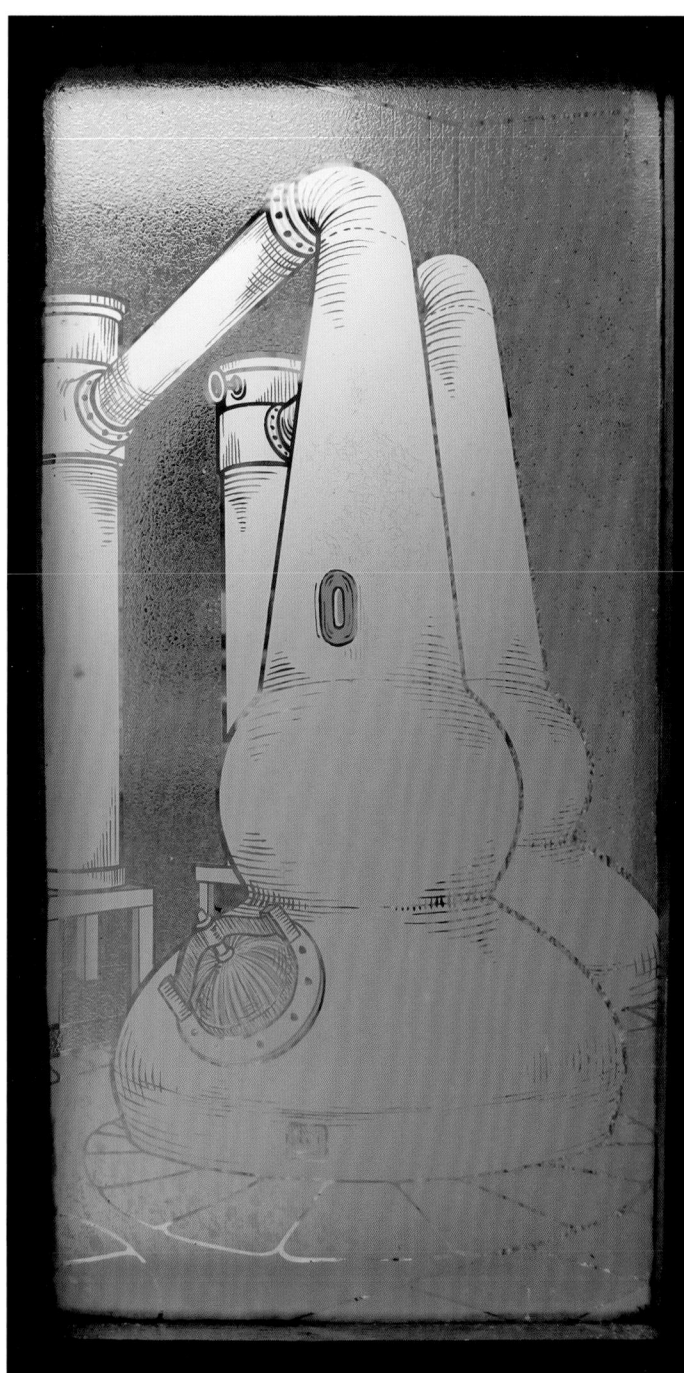

Glendronach Distillery at Forgue near Huntly

Arm wrestling at Huntly Football Club

Ceilidh at Fourteen, Rhynie

An Evening of Scottish and Finnish Music Featuring

Paul Anderson, The Strathspey Fiddlers, Finn Folk Metal Motion and More

ScotFin Ceilidh

In conjunction with the "Room to Roam" festival

Stewarts Hall, Huntly   Friday 9th August   Doors open 7pm

Tickets £5, HDT members £4

Huntly
Development Trust

Foos yer Doos

Singing Group

St Mary's Centre, East End of the High Street, Inverurie

Monday mornings 11 am -12 noon

- Are you, or someone you care for, living with **stroke,**

parkinson's disease, dementia, or **multiple sclerosis*?**

- Would you like to meet others & sing along to music old & new?

- No singing ability required!

- Fully accessible facilities and ample car parking at front.

- Fly cup from around 12noon

- Its Free!

Dufftown Highland Games with Huntly & District Pipe Band's Pipe Major in front

James
Scott Skinner - born in Banchory
known as 'The Strathspey King' -
a name he gave himself. He was a
colourful character - fond of drink &
woman! famous the world over for his
fiddle tunes & being a dance master.

The Tulloch Reel

The meenister kept his
congregation waitin' one could Sunday
and they started tappin' their feet
tae keep warm. And so the tappin'
become a dance and the Tulloch
Reel wis invented.
(The meenister wisnae impressed
though ~~and~~ but the dance became
well known!

Piper Findlater
1st VC awarded in First World War
from Banff.

Piped for a battle - immediately
had his legs shot from under
him but managed to sit on
a rock + pipe for the battle

The late Stanley Robertson once
mistook me as the haunting
piper of the Mill of Tifty

Miguel M. Padilla

ABERDEENSHIRE
THE 'SINGINGSHIRE'

WIND TURBINES:

'They're blowing up bats' lungs.
You can get fined £5000 for
bat killed or displaced.'

'I love them. They're
beautiful. They remind
me of ballerinas'

Fetterangus = Fishie

Local folks clubbing together to
buy a share in a wind turbine.
Puts a whole new slant on
things.

137

Novelty train ride around farm field at BA Stores, Lyne of Skene, Dunecht

Working the land near Troup Head

ANY PERSONS (EXCEPT PLAYERS) CAUGHT COLLECTING GOLF BALLS ON THIS COURSE WILL BE PROSECUTED AND HAVE THEIR BALLS REMOVED.

140   'Gneiss Granite Gabro' artwork in Oldmeldrum inspired by the ancient stone balls, top right; bovine hairball, Aberdeenshire Museums collection, Mintlaw; sign in Huntly Golf Club

Ancient artefacts including flint arrowheads and spindle whorls from the Aberdeenshire Museums Service collection in Mintlaw

Patchwork beast on roundabout in Braemar

Enthroned Santa in Christmas tableau at BA Stores, Dunecht

Tractor drawing by Ewen, Huntly; 'Scottish Samurai' plaque under statue in Fraserburgh; stone outside house in Huntly; sign in Macduff marking distance to Reykjavik

A wild cat was seen in Huntly, Insch + Invenrie 3 yrs ago. It roamed about and it tore a lady's tights. It was after her alright.

'What's that beast there?'
'well it's nae a dog'

Ian McDonald
'it was the size of that cupboard there'

Collecting Aberdeenshire's identity

In October 2013 Aberdeenshire Council commissioned Deveron Arts to develop an artist-led community engagement project to capture the cultural distinctiveness of people and communities across Aberdeenshire. The aim of the project was to identify and express a variety of culturally distinctive characteristics within the region and to inform a branding narrative for which the different communities would take ownership.

In response to this brief, Deveron Arts proposed an artist-led cultural audit for Aberdeenshire in collaboration with artist Jacques Coetzer and The Caravan Gallery (Jan Williams and Chris Teasdale). Aberdeenshire Council assisted us with identifying key stakeholders within the local authority and the wider community. They also provided invaluable support in distributing information about the project and consolidating the data. The main, foremost and chief collective collaborators however were the many diverse people and communities of Aberdeenshire to whom we owe our full gratitude.

Our approach was to undertake a consultation process that was well researched in terms of local history, geography and ethnography, gauging the many communities' opinions and feelings about the area. To begin with the team shortlisted seventeen places that were felt to be most representative of the wide geographic area. Those towns and villages and a range of places along the route were visited over a period of six weeks in the lead up to Christmas. The yellow Caravan Gallery was an iconic catalyst stationed for one or two days in each place where Jan and Chris gathered opinions and sentiments through surveys, a large scale hand drawn map and by simply talking with people on the street. In the meantime, weather and distances permitting, Jacques cycled from place to place to gauge ideas and feelings in between the locations.

This people-centred, street level approach allowed for engagement with people of all ages and social backgrounds to create a dynamic documentation of their responses to Aberdeenshire from a local and personal perspective. For this the team used a combination of photography, video, writings, maps, collections, surveys, interviews and social media to contribute to the bigger picture using information gathered on their travels around the shire.

Claudia Zeiske
Director, Deveron Arts

Deveron Arts

Deveron Arts has no gallery; the town is the venue, research base, studio and stage for artists of all disciplines. We invite them to work and live here from all over the world, engaging with local people and the community in topics of both local and global concern.

Deveron Arts is a contemporary arts organisation based in Huntly, Aberdeenshire. Deveron Arts has an eighteen year track record of engaging with local people and the community through topics of both local and global concern. The resulting artistic and social relationships create a global network that extends throughout and beyond its geographic boundaries.

www.deveron-arts.com

Aberdeenshire Council

Aberdeenshire is a diverse and appealing region with much to make it attractive to those who live here and those who visit. Aberdeenshire Council has been investing in a variety of work in an attempt to describe the cultural distinctiveness of the region. What is it that makes Aberdeenshire recognisably distinct from another region in Scotland or anywhere else, for that matter? Deveron Arts, The Caravan Gallery and Jaques Coetzer have created a picture of Aberdeenshire in the latter part of 2013 through conversations with many people and through capturing images that signify aspects of the character of place.

In their lovely story told here, we see warm, capable and confident people, a tradition of achievement and Aberdeenshire's contribution to the rest of the world.

The pages show our landscapes, outstanding and diverse. They show that there is indeed a good quality of life here as a result of a sense of community and belonging. People who contributed to the project talked about a strong sense of identity with people of integrity tenacity and spirit. We can hear the voices of people who love living here, because it's beautiful, safe and a happy place to live with a strong sense of history and tradition.

Aberdeenshire Council would like to thank the artists who have created this picture of our region and also the 1200 people who took time to give their thoughts and stories to the artists.

Kirsty Duncan
Service Manager, Cultural Services, Lifelong Learning and Leisure, Aberdeenshire Council

ACKNOWLEDGEMENTS

The Artists would like to thank Aberdeenshire Council and Deveron Arts for giving us the opportunity to explore this diverse and underappreciated corner of north east Scotland. Their support is much appreciated.

Thanks also to all the museum staff, arts officers and members of community organisations who assisted us, and to the people of Aberdeenshire for their warm welcome.The stories, songs and opinions they shared with us (once we'd bribed them with delicious shortbread kindly donated by Dean's of Huntly) provided invaluable insights into very different lives across the shire. We are especially grateful to everyone who filled in a survey, wrote on our map or added words, pictures and artefacts to the exhibition in the caravan. Many public contributions are included in this book.

Special thanks also to those individuals who generously gave their time to meet with Jacques in order to share in-depth insights into their particular field. All of these things helped us piece together the jigsaw of contemporary Aberdeenshire.

Jan Williams, Chris Teasdale and Jacques Coetzer

Published by Aberdeenshire Council
© Aberdeenshire Council 2014
ISBN 978-0-9929334-2-5
All rights reserved.

www.thecaravangallery.photography
Facebook: The Caravan Gallery
Twitter @caravangallery

http://www.jacquescoetzer.co.za

Aberdeenshire Ways branding, Geddes and local / global theme, icons and photographs on pages 13, 14, 15, 16 (left) , 11, 110, 115, 117, 132, 133 by Jacques Coetzer.

Photographs by The Caravan Gallery unless otherwise stated.

Book design: The Caravan Gallery and IDProjects.

MIX
Paper from responsible sources
FSC® C014841